# 120 Great
# Fairy Paintings

### Edited by
### Jeff Menges

**Dover Publications, Inc.**
Mineola, New York

The CD-ROM in this book contains all of the images. Each image has been saved in 300-dpi high-quality JPEG and 72-dpi Internet-ready JPEG formats. There is no installation necessary. Just insert the CD into your computer and call the images into your favorite software (refer to the documentation with your software for further instructions).

Within the Images folder on the CD, you will find two additional folders—"Large JPG" and "JPG. " Every image has a unique file name in the following format: xxx.JPG. The first 3 digits of the file name, before the period, correspond to the number printed under the image in the book. The last 3 characters of the file name, "JPG," refer to the file format. So, 001.JPG would be the first file in the folder.

Also included on the CD-ROM is Dover Design Manager, a simple graphics editing program for Windows that will allow you to view, print, crop, and rotate the images.

For technical support, contact:
 Telephone: 1 (617) 249-0245
 Fax: 1 (617) 249-0245
 Email: dover@artimaging.com
 Internet: **http://www.dovertechsupport.com**
 The fastest way to receive technical support is via email or the Internet.

*Bibliographical Note*

*120 Great Fairy Paintings CD-ROM and Book* is a new work, first published by Dover Publications, Inc., in 2006.

## Dover Full-Color Electronic Design Series®

*International Standard Book Number: 0-486-99741-3*

Manufactured in the United States of America
Dover Publications, Inc., 31 East 2nd Street, Mineola, N.Y. 11501

001. HENRY FUSELI
*Titania's Awakening,* 1785–89

002. HENRY FUSELI
*Titania and Bottom,* c.1790

003. WILLIAM BLAKE
*Oberon, Titania and Puck with Fairies Dancing*, c. 1785

004. JOHN LAMB 'PRIMUS'
*A Midsummer Night's Dream*, 1834

006. DANIEL MACLISE
Undine and the Wood Demon, 1843

007. RICHARD DADD
*Puck*, 1841

008. RICHARD DADD
*Titania Sleeping*, c. 1841

010. RICHARD DADD
*Come Unto These Yellow Sands*, 1842

011. RICHARD DADD
*Contradiction: Oberon and Titania, 1854–58)*

012. RICHARD DADD
*The Fairy Feller's Master Stroke, 1855–64*

013. GEORGE CRUIKSHANK, JR.
*A Fairy Dance,* n.d.

014. FREDERICK HOWARD MICHAEL
*Titania,* 1896

015. JOSEPH NOEL PATON
*The Reconciliation of Oberon and Titania*, 1847

016. JOSEPH NOEL PATON
*The Quarrel of Oberon and Titania*, 1849

017. JOSEPH NOEL PATON
*Puck and the Fairy,* n.d.

018. JOSEPH NOEL PATON
*Under the Sea I,* n.d.

019. JOSEPH NOEL PATON
*Under the Sea II*, n.d.

020  JOSEPH NOEL PATON
*The Fairy Queen*, c. 1860

021. RICHARD DOYLE
*In Fairyland: Rehearsal in Fairyland,* 1870

022. RICHARD DOYLE
*In Fairyland: The Fairy Queen Takes an Airy Drive,* 1870

023. RICHARD DOYLE
*In Fairyland: Asleep in the Moonlight,* 1870

024. RICHARD DOYLE
*In Fairyland,* 1870, fairy with owls

025. RICHARD DOYLE
*In Fairyland,* 1870, fairies playing with a robin

026. RICHARD DOYLE
*In Fairyland,* 1870, fairies and waterlilies

027. RICHARD DOYLE
*In Fairyland,* 1870, a fairy kiss

028. RICHARD DOYLE
*The Attar Cup in Aagerup—the Moment of Departure,* n.d.

029. RICHARD DOYLE
*The Fairy Tree,* n.d.

030. RICHARD DOYLE
*Wood Elves Hiding and Watching a Lady,* n.d.

031. RICHARD DOYLE
*Under the Dock Leaves: An Autumnal Evening's Dream*, 1878

032. RICHARD DOYLE
*The God Thor and the Dwarves*, 1878

033. CHARLES ALTAMONT DOYLE
*A Dance Around the Moon,* n.d.

034. JOHN ANSTER FITZGERALD
*The Captive Dreamer,* 1856

035. JOHN ANSTER FITZGERALD
*The Artist's Dream*, 1857

036. JOHN ANSTER FITZGERALD
*The Stuff that Dreams Are Made Of*, c. 1858

038. JOHN ANSTER FITZGERALD
*Ariel*, c.1858

040. JOHN ANSTER FITZGERALD
*Fairy Musicians, n.d.*

039. JOHN ANSTER FITZGERALD
*The Birds Nest, n.d.*

041. JOHN ANSTER FITZGERALD
*Fairies Attacking a Bat*, n.d.

042. JOHN ANSTER FITZGERALD
*The Enchanted Forest*, n.d.

043. JOHN ANSTER FITZGERALD
*Robin Defending His Nest*, c. 1858–60

044. JOHN ANSTER FITZGERALD
*The Fledgling*, n.d.

045. JOHN ANSTER FITZGERALD
*The Fairies' Banquet, 1859*

046. JOHN ANSTER FITZGERALD
*The Fairy's Barque, 1860*

047. JOHN ANSTER FITZGERALD
*Who Killed Cock Robin?,* n.d.

048. JOHN ANSTER FITZGERALD
*The Fairy Falconer,* n.d.

049. JOHN ANSTER FITZGERALD
*Titania and Bottom*, a scene from *A Midsummer Night's Dream*, n.d.

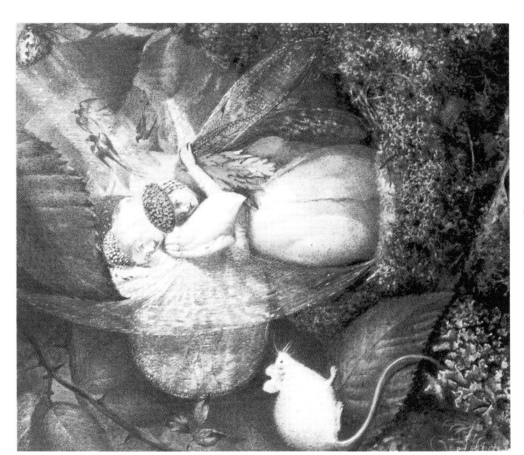

050. JOHN ANSTER FITZGERALD
*Fairy Lovers in a Bird's Nest*, c.1860

051. JOHN ANSTER FITZGERALD
*The Fairy's Funeral*, 1864

052. JOHN ANSTER FITZGERALD
*The Captive Robin*, n.d.

053. JOHN ANSTER FITZGERALD
*Fairies Looking Through a Gothic Arch*, c.1864

054. FRANCIS DANBY
*Fairies by a Rocky Stream*, n.d.

055. FRANCIS DANBY
*Scene from A Midsummer Night's Dream, 1832*

056. JOHN GEORGE NAISH
*Titania, n.d.*

057 JOHN GEORGE NAISH
*Moon Fairies II, 1853*

058. JOHN GEORGE NAISH
*Elves and Fairies: A Midsummer Night's Dream, 1856*

059. STEPHEN REID
*A Midsmmer Night's Dream*, (1907)

060. ADELAIDE CLAXTON
*Wonderland*, n.d.

061. EDMUND THOMAS PARRIS
The Visit at Moonlight (1832)

062. EDWARD HENRY CORBOULD
*A Fairy Scene, Rothkäppchen*, 1855

063. ROBERT ALEXANDER HILLINGFORD
*The Fairy Dance,* n.d.

064. THEODORE VON HOLST
*Fairy Lovers,* c. 1840

065. EDWIN HENRY LANDSEER
*Scene from A Midsummer Night's Dream, Titania and Bottom, 1848–51*

066. ROBERT HUSKISSON
*The Midsummer Night's Fairies, 1847*

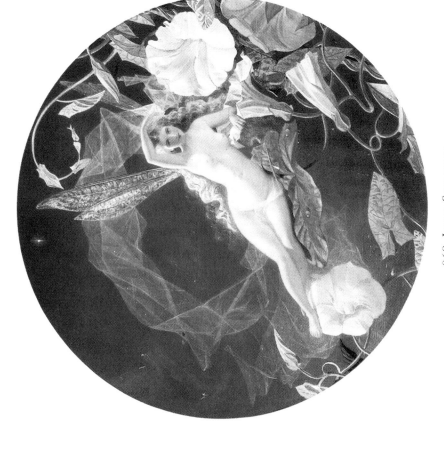

068. JOHN SIMMONS
*Fairy Lying on a Leaf*, n.d.

067. JOHN SIMMONS
*The Honey Bags Steal from the Humble Bees*, n.d.

069. JOHN SIMMONS
*The Evening Star*, n.d.

070. JOHN SIMMONS
*Titania*, 1866

072. Kate Cameron
*Joy*, 1892

071. John Simmons
*A Midsummer Night's Dream: Hermia and the Fairies*, 1861

073. THOMAS MAYBANK
*Come Unto These Yellow Sands, 1906*

074. ESTALLA CANZIANI
*The Piper of Dreams, 1914*

075. ETHELINE E. DELL
*Midsummer Fairies*, c. 1885

076. WALTER JENKS MORGAN
*Where Rural Fays and Fairies Dwell*, c.1900

077. Thomas Heatherly
*The Golden Age*, c.1862

078. Arthur Rackham
*Elfin Revellers*, 1900

080. ARTHUR RACKHAM
*A Midsummer Night's Dream: "She never had so sweet a changeling," 1908*

079. ARTHUR RACKHAM
*Dancing with the Fairies, 1906*

082. ARTHUR RACKHAM

*A Midsummer Night's Dream: "Fairies away!",* 1908

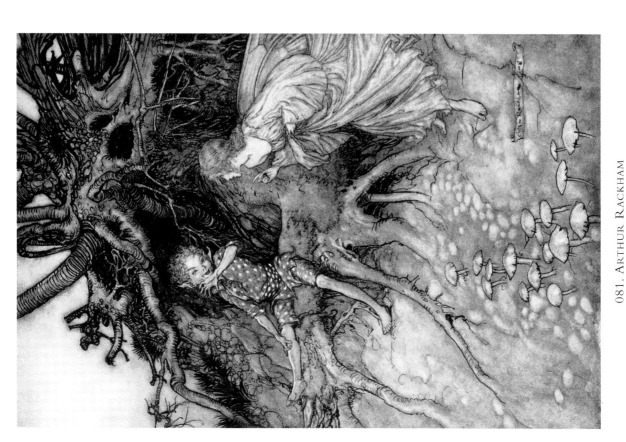

081. ARTHUR RACKHAM

*A Midsummer Night's Dream: "I am that merry wanderer of the night,"* 1908

084. ARTHUR RACKHAM
*A Midsummer Night's Dream:* "One aloof stand sentinel," 1908

083. ARTHUR RACKHAM
*A Midsummer Night's Dream:* "And a fairy song," 1908

086. ARTHUR RACKHAM
*Arthur Rackham's Book of Pictures: The Magic Cup*, 1913

085. ARTHUR RACKHAM
*A Midsummer Night's Dream:* "And her fairy sent
To bear him to my bower in fairy land," 1908

088. EDMUND DULAC

*Beauty and the Beast: "She found herself face to face
with a stately and beautiful lady," 1910*

087. ARTHUR RACKHAM

*Comus: "Sabrina rises, attended by water-Nymphs," 1921*

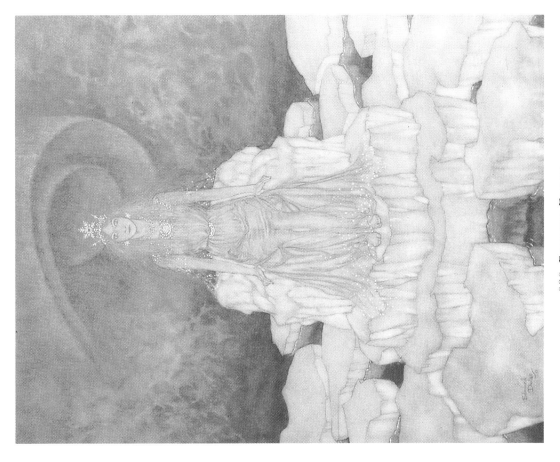

090. EDMUND DULAC
*The Snow Queen, 1911*

089. EDMUND DULAC
*The Snow Queen,* "One day he was in a high state of delight.," 1911

092. EDMUND DULAC

*The Garden of Paradise: "The Fairy of the Garden now advanced to meet them," 1911*

091. EDMUND DULAC

*The Garden of Paradise: "The Eagle in the great Forest flew swiftly,*
*but the Eastwing flew more swiftly still," 1911*

094. WARWICK GOBLE
*The Water Babies: "He watched the moonlight on the rippling river," 1910*

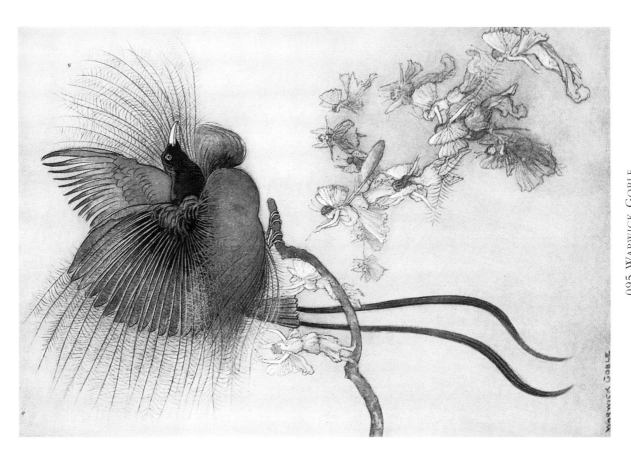

096. WARWICK GOBLE
*Stories from the Pentamerone: "The Fairy Appearing to the Prince," 1911*

098. WARWICK GOBLE
*Book of Fairy Poetry:* "And, sweetly singing round about thy bed," 1920

097. WARWICK GOBLE
*The Fairy Book:* "The fairy there welcomed her majesty," 1913

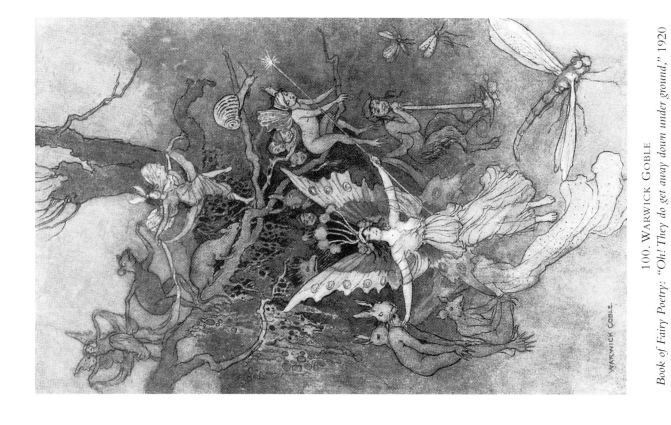

100. WARWICK GOBLE
*Book of Fairy Poetry:* "*Oh! They do get away down under ground,*" 1920

099. WARWICK GOBLE
*Book of Fairy Poetry:* "*Buy from us with a golden curl,*" 1920

102. WARWICK GOBLE
*Book of Fairy Poetry:* "*Instead of crust a peacock pie,*" 1920

101. WARWICK GOBLE
*Book of Fairy Poetry:* "*Three spirits mad with joy,*" 1920

104. WARWICK GOBLE

*Book of Fairy Poetry: "Wake, when some vile thing is near," 1920*

103. WARWICK GOBLE

*Book of Fairy Poetry: "Sea-nymphs hourly ring his knell," 1920*

106. WARWICK GOBLE
Book of Fairy Poetry: "Off, ye icy Spirits, fly," 1920

105. WARWICK GOBLE
Book of Fairy Poetry: "For the Nautilus is my boat," 1920

108. WARWICK GOBLE

*Book of Fairy Poetry: "And the padding feet of many gnomes a-coming," 1920*

107. WARWICK GOBLE

*Book of Fairy Poetry: "But Puck was seated on a spider's thread," 1920*

110. JOHN DUNCAN
*The Riders of the Sidhe*, 1911

111. JOHN ATKINSON GRIMSHAW
*Iris, Spirit of the Rainbow*, 1876

112. JOHN ATKINSON GRIMSHAW
*Spirit of the Night*, 1879

113. JOHN ATKINSON GRIMSHAW
*Autumn*, n.d.

114. EDWARD ROBERT HUGHES
*Midsummer Eve*, 1908

115. EDWARD ROBERT HUGHES
*Twilight Fantasies,* 1911

116. SOPHIE ANDERSON
*Take the Fair Face of Woman.* c. 1869

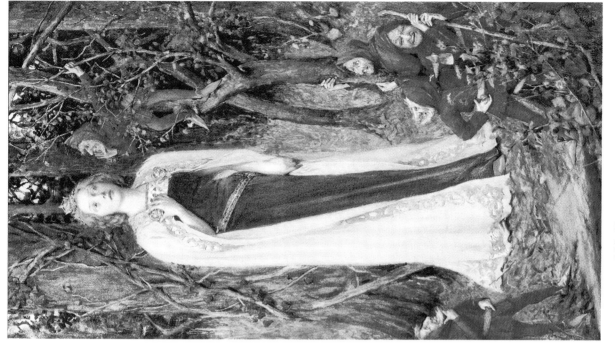

118. Henry Meynell Rheam
*Once Upon a Time, n.d.*

117. John Everett Millais
*Ferdinand Lured by Ariel, 1849*

119. Henry Meynell Rheam
*The Fairy Woods*, 1903

120. Helen Jacobs
*The Fairy Jewels*, 1912

# LIST OF ARTISTS